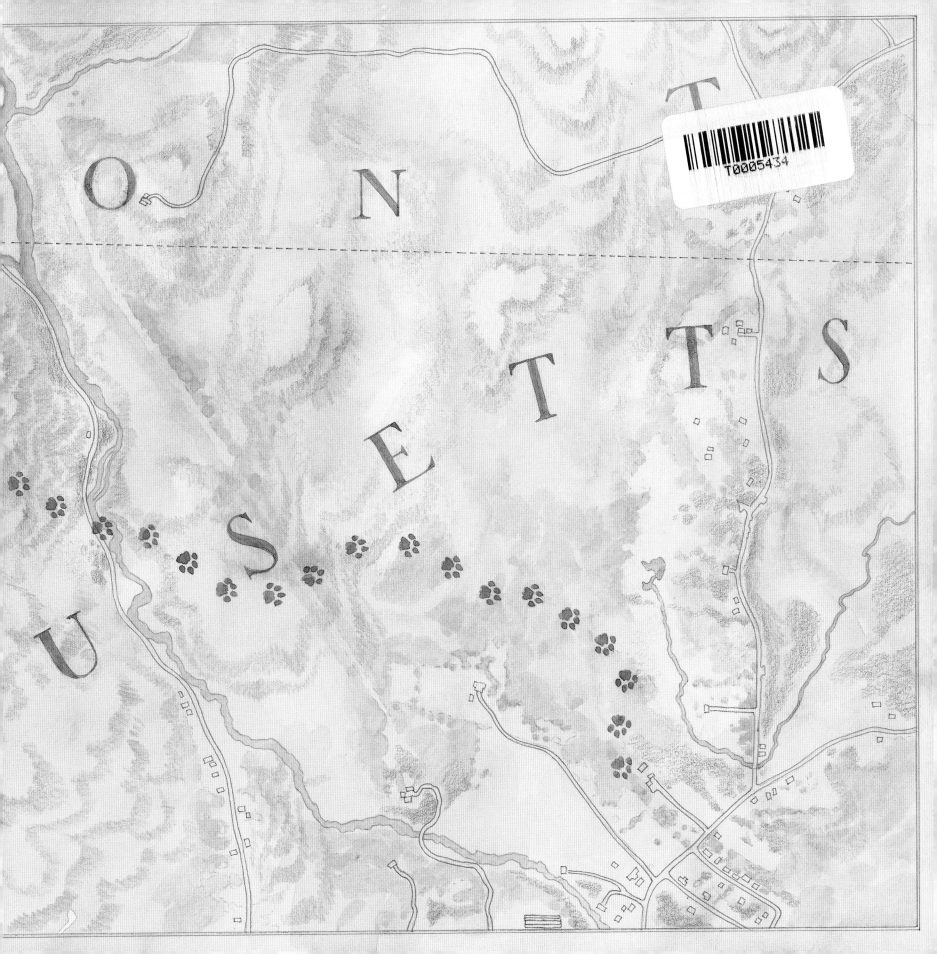

BOBCAT PROWLING

Maria Gianferrari

Pictures by **Bagram Ibatoulline**

ROARING BROOK PRESS

New York

Published by Roaring Brook Press
Roaring Brook Press is a division of Holtzbrinck Publishing Holdings Limited Partnership
120 Broadway, New York, NY 10271 • mackids.com

Library of Congress Control Number: 2021917033
ISBN 978-1-62672-786-1

Our books may be purchased in bulk for promotional, educational, or business use.
Please contact your local bookseller or the Macmillan Corporate and Premium Sales Department
at (800) 221-7945 ext. 5442 or by email at MacmillanSpecialMarkets@macmillan.com.

First edition, 2022
Printed in China by RR Donnelley Asia Printing Solutions Ltd., Dongguan City, Guangdong Province

1 3 5 7 9 10 8 6 4 2

ABOUT THIS BOOK The illustrations for this book were created with watercolors.
This book was edited by Emily Feinberg and designed by Angela Jun with art direction by Neil Swaab.
The production was supervised by Susan Doran, and the production editor was Allyson Floridia.
The text was set in Adobe Jensen Pro, and the display type is Mixed Breed.

For Joan, agent extraordinaire, as elegant as a bobcat,
on the hunt to find homes for my books —M.G.

To my dear friend Kura, an animal lover
—B.I.

Beyond your house,
behind tall pines,
under paling stars
Mother Bobcat wakes.

Bobcat Yearling,
from last year's litter,
stretches and yawns.

You touch their tracks in the snow.

A caterwaul pierces the air,
and Mother Bobcat tenses,
then growls in return.
It's time for Mother Bobcat to mate,
then raise this season's kittens.

Mother Bobcat hisses and swipes at Yearling,
driving him away.
Yearling must find a home range of his own.

Yearling's journey will be a long one.
Resident bobcats surround his
mother's territory.

Yearling travels on train tracks.
Bitter winds flatten his fur.
Ice crusts between his toes.
He shelters under spruces
shawled with snow.

Yearling wakes and shakes.
Could this be his new home?
Yearling sniffs.
Pellets trail to a grove of beech and maple.
Yearling tracks.
Snowshoe Hare nibbles fallen twigs.
Crusted snow cracks.

Snowshoe Hare shudders.

JUMP!

Canada Lynx glides on snowshoe paws,
seizing his prey.
This is Lynx's territory.
Yearling must move on.

Dawn blushes.
Stars dim.
A belt of oaks circles a beaver pond.
Could this be Yearling's new home?
Yearling stalks Squirrel . . .

LEAp!

Resident Bobcat growls and charges,
snatching Squirrel.
This is his home.
Yearling must move on.

Yearling wanders.
Winter wanes.
You watch from your window
as Yearling visits your bird feeder,
snaring unsuspecting songbirds.
But he's just passing through.

Yearling treks along a riverbank.
Ring-necked pheasants forage,
scratching the soil.
Could this be Yearling's new home?

Yearling is hungry,
but he must be patient.
His spotted coat
keeps him camouflaged.
His retracted claws
stay sharp in their sheaths
and help him silently stalk.
Wait.
Crouch.

STRIKE!

Pheasants scatter.

Yearling retreats to feed,
but not for long.
A-WOOO!

This is Coyote's territory.
Yearling sprints,
but Coyote is close behind.
Yearling races up the red maple,
dropping Pheasant.

Coyote eats and waits,
waits and eats.
But he's not as patient as Yearling . . .

Now napping under the stars.

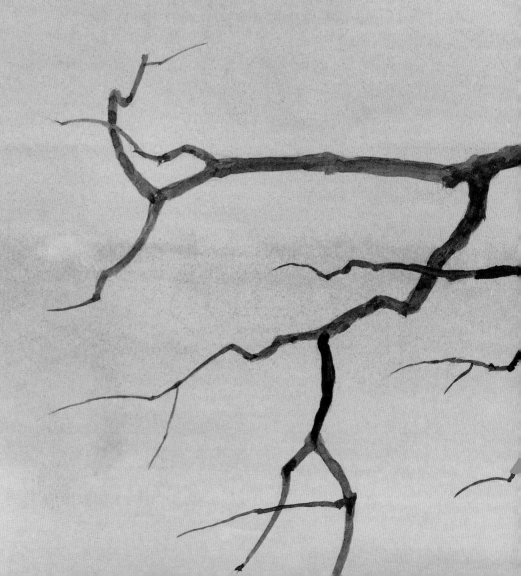

Constellations have come
and gone.

Yearling has roamed so many miles,
he's now a Bobcat.

Dogwoods open;
mountain laurels bloom
like spring snowflakes.

A ribbon of road stretches
between houses,
and Bobcat follows it.
At the side of the road lies Old Bobcat.
Bobcat sniffs, rakes trees with his claws,
scrapes soil, and sprays,
marking his territory.

Bobcat spots Cottontail.

SPRING!

Cottontail flushes,
zigzagging through your backyard,
but Bobcat is faster.

You peek from your porch.

Bobcat will eat, then rest.
His journey has been long,
but now he's home.

This is your home, too.
And tonight,
you will sleep under the stars.
Just like Bobcat.

ALL ABOUT BOBCATS

BOBCATS are about twice the size of an average house cat and are named for their stubby, six-inch tails.

Bobcat babies are called **KITTENS**. A female bobcat has a litter averaging three kittens. Kittens learn to hunt at around five months of age. They live with their mother for at least nine months, but sometimes as long as two years.

YOUNG BOBCATS one to two years old are called yearlings. When yearlings leave their mother to find their own home range, it's called dispersal.

Bobcats **LIVE** all over North America: from the Atlantic to the Pacific coast, and from southern Canada into central Mexico.

Bobcats live in all kinds of **HABITATS**: swamps, mountains, deserts, forests, and wooded areas bordering suburbs. They seek ledges and cliffs as refuges for resting, raising kittens, and escaping from predators.

A **HOME RANGE** is a territory where a bobcat hunts, travels, rests, and rears its young. Bobcats living in a home range are called residents. The yearling in this story is a transient bobcat searching for his own home range. Transient bobcats may have to travel many miles to find available territory. A bobcat marks its territory by making scent trails. It has special glands around its mouth, cheeks, and chin; between its toes; and on and under its tail. The scents are released when a bobcat rubs its head on an object, claws a tree, or makes scrapes (scratching the soil and spraying it with urine or scat). These scents say: *Stay away! This is my home!*

CANADA LYNXES, cousins to bobcats, live in the northern regions of the United States and in Canada. Their furry footpads spread out like snowshoes to help them walk on snow and capture their favorite prey, the snowshoe hare.

Bobcat **BODIES** are made for hunting. Their spotted coats camouflage them from prey. Their retractable claws and the webbed skin and fur between their toes muffle the sound of the cats' creeping. Longer hind legs help them leap, and sharp claws spring out like switchblades to seize their prey. Their scissorlike teeth are as sharp as knives, and their barbed tongues remove meat from bones. They hunt by stalking and ambushing their prey.

Bobcats are **CREPUSCULAR HUNTERS**, meaning they're most active at dusk and dawn, just like their prey. In the winter or when they're looking for territory, like the yearling in this story, they move about during daylight hours.

Bobcats are **SPRINTERS**—they can run the hundred-yard dash in under ten seconds! Their bodies are built for short chases. If they don't catch their prey within sixty feet, they give up the chase. Although they're only around three feet long, bobcats can jump more than ten feet long and eight feet high.

COVER such as stands of trees, bushes, grasses, and brush are areas where bobcats can stalk, hide, rest, and retreat from bad weather. Cover also provides protection for prey animals.

What's a bobcat's favorite **ACTIVITY**? Inactivity! They rest, nap, sleep, and loll around in lookouts. It's even one of their hunting strategies.

HOW TO HUNT LIKE A BOBCAT

1. **Look**: Seek cover—areas for hiding and stalking, like tall grasses, bushes, hedges, or brush.

2. **Watch**: Your vision is keen. Your eyes are bigger than the eyes of most carnivores. They face forward and are close together—this lets you judge how close your prey is.

3. **Stalk**: Your retractable claws help you stalk silently; your spotted coat helps you blend in.

4. **Wait**: Get as close to your prey as possible. Surprise is your best weapon.

5. **Crouch**: Spring! Your longer hind legs help you leap through the air and seize your prey with your sharp claws.

6. **Chase**: If you miss on the first try, give chase. You're built for speed—your muscular legs and flexible spine give you a long stride.

7. **Nap**: If your prey escapes, find a lookout near a food or water source and take a nap. Your meal will come to you.

8. **Repeat**: Between resting periods, repeat beginning with Step 2.

WHAT'S ON THE MENU?

Meat! Bobcats are carnivores. Ninety percent of their diet is made up of cottontail rabbits, snowshoe hares, and jackrabbits. But the daily special depends on the bobcat's habitat as well as the season. Bobcats in the north, especially males, dine on deer (usually fawns or weak does) when there is deep snow. In the southwestern desert, lizards or snakes might be their main course. Southeastern swamp dwellers snack on snakes, rats, and waterfowl. Rodents and rabbits, beware! Rodents such as rats, mice, voles, groundhogs, and squirrels make quick and easy appetizers. A mother bobcat and her three kittens can eat thousands of rats and mice and nearly a thousand rabbits in just one year! Bobcats also feast on birds, bats, opossums, and even domestic animals such as chickens, goats, and sheep. Because they eat so many different foods, bobcats can live in all kinds of places.

Further reading

Hansen, Kevin. *Bobcat: Master of Survival*. New York: Oxford University Press, 2007.

Kobalenko, Jerry. *Forest Cats of North America: Cougars, Bobcats, Lynx*. Buffalo, NY: Firefly Books, 1997.

Squire, Ann O. *Bobcats (A True Book)*. New York: Children's Press, 2005.

Swinburne, Stephen R. *Bobcat: North America's Cat*. Honesdale, PA: Boyds Mills Press, 2001.

Websites and videos

Animal Diversity Web: animaldiversity.org/accounts/Lynx_rufus

Bobcat City—Studying Urban Cats, Texas Parks and Wildlife: youtube.com/watch?v=0mbGhS9ZNhQ

Bobcat Kitten Hunting Lesson—America's National Parks, National Geographic:
    youtube.com/watch?v=kuBR6quGWyQ

Does the bobcat make it?: youtube.com/watch?v=fmTn6hLRm7s&t=2s

National Geographic: animals.nationalgeographic.com/animals/mammals/bobcat

National Geographic Kids: kids.nationalgeographic.com/animals/mammals/facts/bobcat

NatureWorks: nhptv.org/natureworks/bobcat.htm

Washington Department of Fish and Wildlife: wdfw.wa.gov/living/bobcats.html

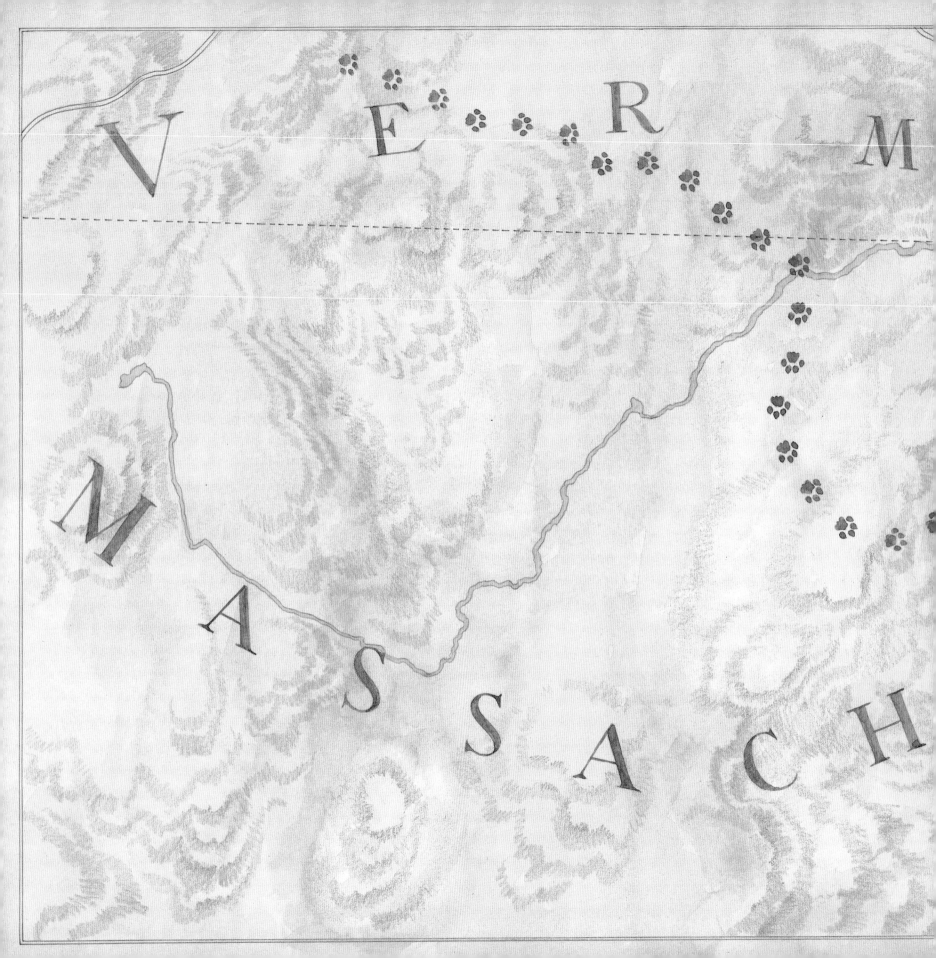